Team Spirit

THE ARIZONA DIAMONDBACKS

BY
MARK STEWART

Content Consultant
James L. Gates, Jr.
Library Director
National Baseball Hall of Fame and Museum

NORWOOD HOUSE PRESS
CHICAGO, ILLINOIS

BALDWIN PUBLIC LIBRARY

Norwood House Press
P.O. Box 316598
Chicago, Illinois 60631

For information regarding Norwood House Press, please visit our website at:
www.norwoodhousepress.com or call 866-565-2900.

All photos courtesy of Getty Images except the following:
Topps, Inc. (14, 22 bottom, 40 top & bottom left);
Black Book archives (40 bottom).
Cover photo by Greg Flume/Getty Images.
Special thanks to Topps, Inc.

Editor: Mike Kennedy
Designer: Ron Jaffe
Project Management: Black Book Partners, LLC.
Special thanks to Dwayne, Heather, and Matthew Morrison.

Library of Congress Cataloging-in-Publication Data

Stewart, Mark, 1960-
  The Arizona Diamondbacks / by Mark Stewart ; content consultant, James L.
Gates, Jr.
       p. cm. -- (Team spirit)
   Summary: "Presents the history, accomplishments and key personalities of the Arizona Diamondbacks baseball team. Includes timelines, quotes, maps, glossary and websites"--Provided by publisher.
   Includes bibliographical references and index.
   ISBN-13: 978-1-59953-163-2 (library edition : alk. paper)
   ISBN-10: 1-59953-163-1 (library edition : alk. paper) 1. Arizona Diamondbacks (Baseball team)--History--Juvenile literature. I. Gates, James L. II. Title.
GV875.A64S74 2008
796.357'640975965--dc22
                                                                          2007043502

© 2008 by Norwood House Press.
All rights reserved.
No part of this book may be reproduced without written permission from the publisher.

•

The Arizona Diamondbacks is a registered trademark of Arizona Professional Baseball LP.
Major League Baseball trademarks and copyrights are used
with permission of Major League Baseball Properties, Inc.

Manufactured in the United States of America.

COVER PHOTO: The Diamondbacks slap high fives after a win during the 2007 season.

Table of Contents

CHAPTER	PAGE
Meet the Diamondbacks	4
Way Back When	6
The Team Today	10
Home Turf	12
Dressed for Success	14
We Won!	16
Go-To Guys	20
On the Sidelines	24
One Great Day	26
Legend Has It	28
It Really Happened	30
Team Spirit	32
Timeline	34
Fun Facts	36
Talking Baseball	38
For the Record	40
Pinpoints	42
Play Ball	44
Glossary	46
Places to Go	47
Index	48

SPORTS WORDS & VOCABULARY WORDS: In this book, you will find many words that are new to you. You may also see familiar words used in new ways. The glossary on page 46 gives the meanings of baseball words, as well as "everyday" words that have special baseball meanings. These words appear in **bold type** throughout the book. The glossary on page 47 gives the meanings of vocabulary words that are not related to baseball. They appear in ***bold italic type*** throughout the book.

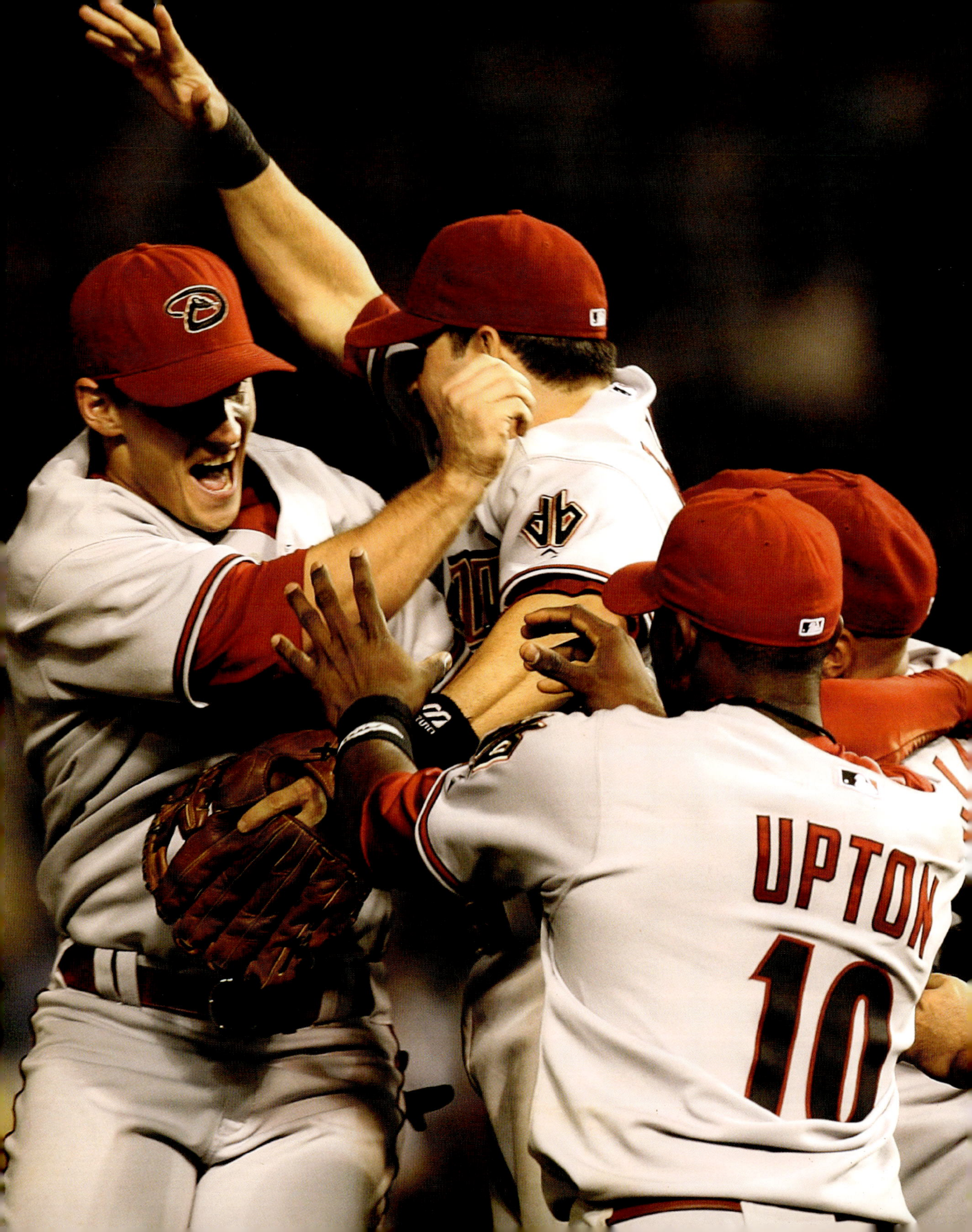
UPTON
10

Meet the Diamondbacks

There are different ways of building a winning baseball team. One way is to put together a group of **experienced** stars and then fill in around them with helpful younger players. Another way is to discover talented **prospects**, teach them what it takes to win, and then surround them with helpful older players. The Arizona Diamondbacks have done both.

The Diamondbacks are one of the newest teams in sports, but they are old pros when it comes to winning. A smart manager, a handful of bright stars, and a lot of team spirit can add up to a championship.

This book tells the story of the Diamondbacks. They joined the **National League (NL)** in 1998 and built a **tradition** of success right from the start. They won over a lot of people in baseball who **insisted** a new team must wait to win. More important, they won the hearts of millions of fans in the baseball-hungry Southwest.

The Diamondbacks jump for joy after finishing in first place in 2007.

Way Back When

A few weeks before the 1995 baseball season began, the owners voted to add two new teams for the 1998 season. Three years later, the Arizona Diamondbacks and Tampa Bay Devil Rays became the 29th and 30th teams in the big leagues. The Diamondbacks were named after a species of rattlesnake that lives in the deserts of the American Southwest.

The team's main owner was Jerry Colangelo. He also owned the Phoenix Suns basketball team. Colangelo's partners included Phillip Knight, who owned Nike, comedian Billy Crystal, and basketball star Danny Manning. The "D-backs" struggled in their first season and finished last in the **NL West**. Their best players in 1998 were **veterans** Matt Williams, Jay Bell, Devon White, and Andy Benes.

Arizona fans were willing to be *patient* with the Diamondbacks, but the owners were not as willing. Over the winter, they added **starting pitcher** Randy Johnson and a whole new outfield of Luis Gonzalez, Steve Finley, and Tony Womack. The Diamondbacks won 100 games in just their second season—something no **expansion team** had ever done.

Over the next two seasons, the Diamondbacks welcomed several more experienced stars. Mark Grace, Reggie Sanders, Craig Counsell, Curt Schilling, and Miguel Batista joined Arizona, and the team captured the 2001 NL **pennant**. Johnson went 21–6 and was his league's best pitcher. Gonzalez also had an amazing year. He hit 57 home runs and had 142 **runs batted in (RBI)**.

The 2001 **World Series** helped America recover from the shock and sadness of the September 11th terrorist attacks. The Diamondbacks played the New York Yankees in seven dramatic games. Arizona won

LEFT: Jerry Colangelo
ABOVE: Luis Gonzalez takes a big swing during the 2001 season.

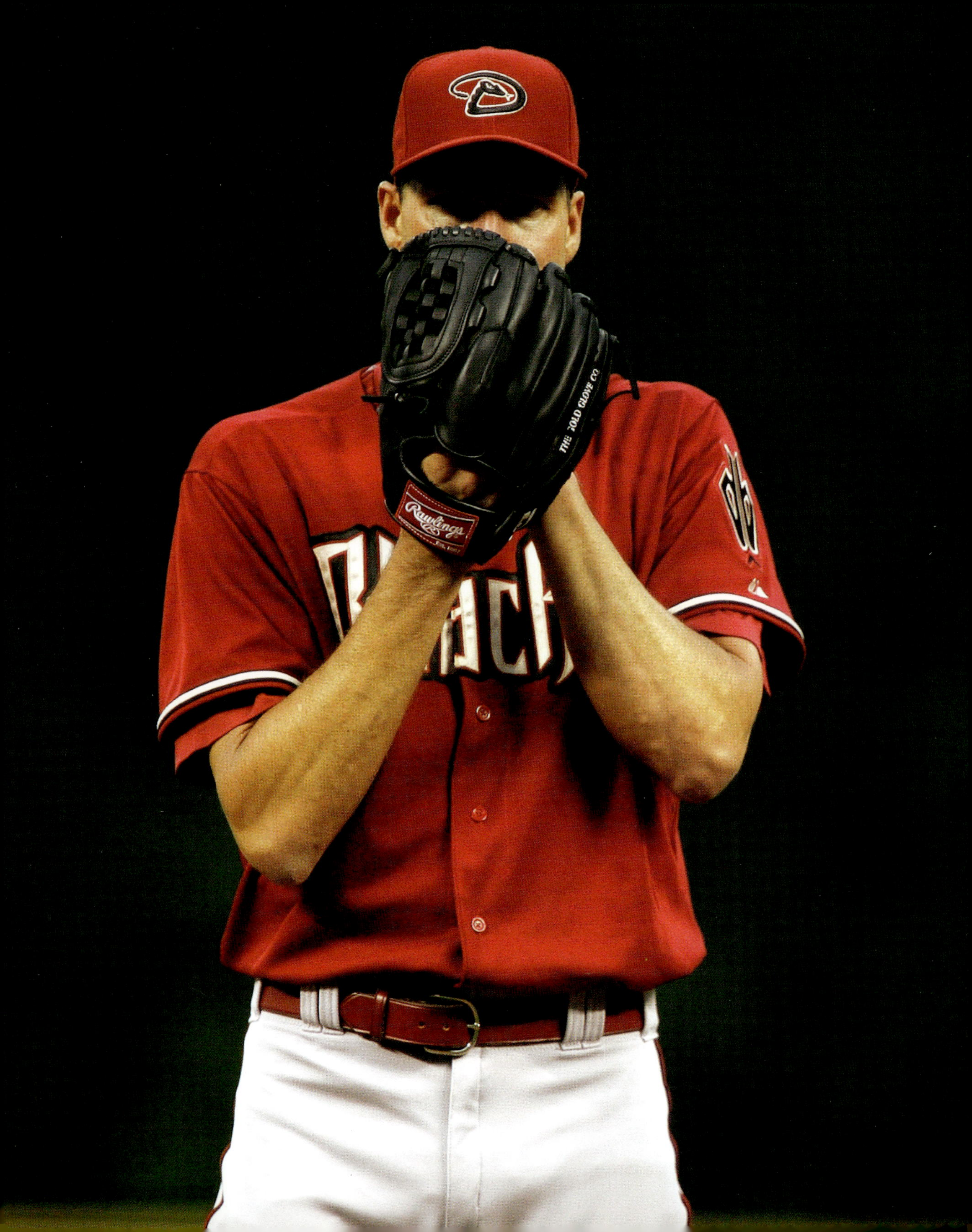
THE GOLD GLOVE CO.
Rawlings

the championship in the last inning of the final game. Johnson and Schilling shared honors as the series **Most Valuable Player (MVP)**. With their title, the Diamondbacks reminded fans that playing hard and having fun was a great recipe for victory.

The Diamondbacks won the NL West again in 2002, but they did not return to the World Series. Johnson and Schilling again *dominated* on the mound. Gonzalez, Finley, and Womack continued to lead the offense.

Unfortunately, the Diamondbacks began to feel the effects of age and injuries. In 2004, the team decided to rebuild around a new *generation* of players. The first of those prospects to make it big was Brandon Webb, a pitcher who developed into a star. But the fans in Arizona still had to be patient—many of the talented young Diamondbacks were little more than teenagers. As Arizona would soon discover, however, these kids were worth the wait!

LEFT: Randy Johnson looks in for a sign from the catcher.
ABOVE: Curt Schilling formed a great one-two pitching punch with Johnson for the Diamondbacks.

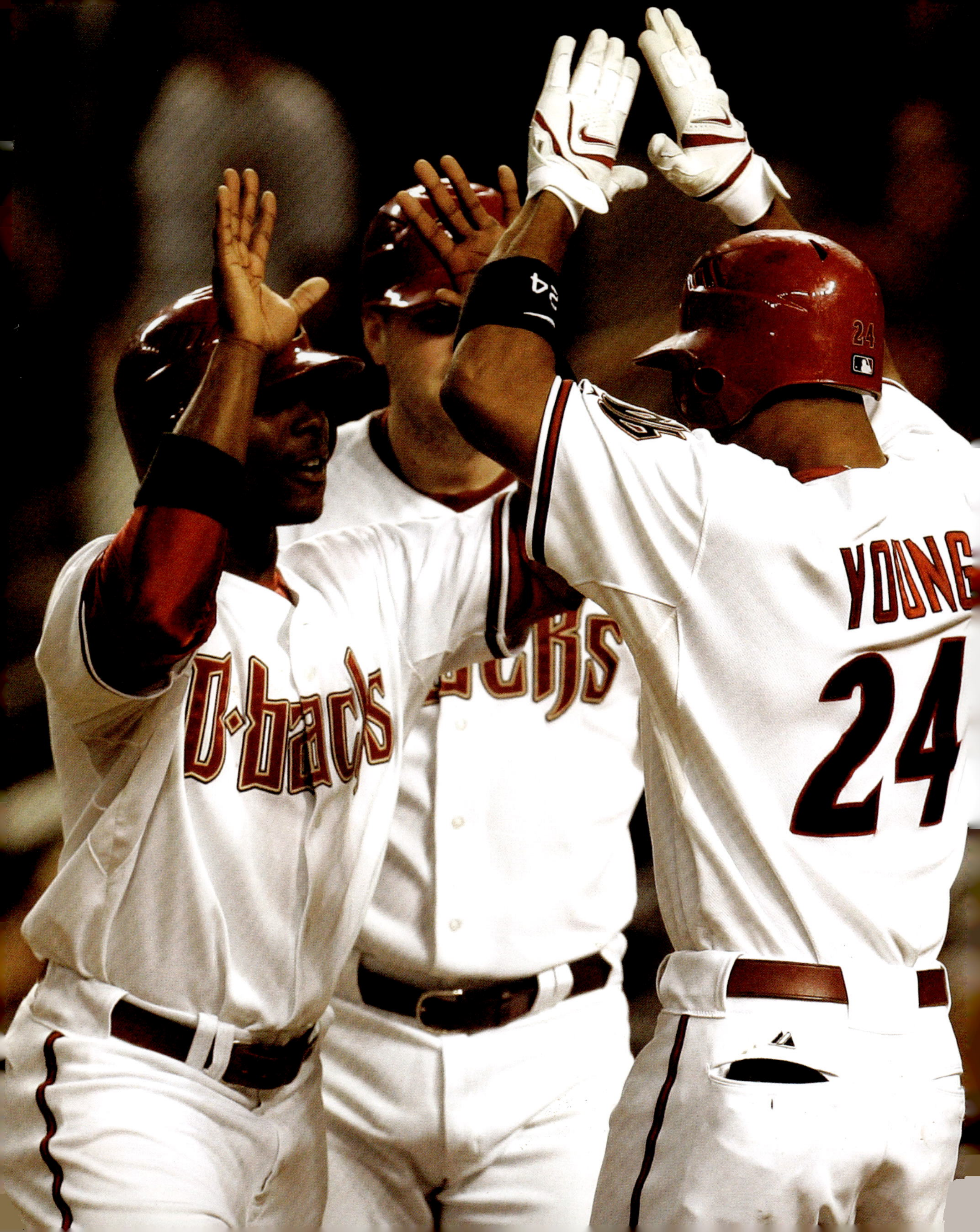
D-backs
YOUNG
24

The Team Today

The Diamondbacks won their first championship with older players who knew how to win. When Arizona set its sights on a second championship, the team decided to use a different *strategy*. This time, the Diamondbacks would rely on a group of younger players.

By 2007, some of baseball's brightest rising stars were wearing the Arizona uniform. Conor Jackson, Stephen Drew, Chad Tracy, Chris Young, Micah Owings, Justin Upton, Mark Reynolds, Miguel Montero, Edgar Gonzalez, Jose Valverde, and Carlos Quentin "grew up" together in the **minor leagues**.

These youngsters joined experienced stars such as Brandon Webb, Eric Byrnes, Orlando Hudson, and Livan Hernandez. Together, they finished first in the NL West. The Diamondbacks have become one of baseball's most exciting teams. Their players have learned to win games in many different ways.

Justin Upton and Chris Young congratulate each other during the 2007 season. They are two of the promising young players who helped lead Arizona back to the top of baseball.

APS
PEPSI
Miller Lite
US AIRWAYS
THE ARIZONA REPUBLIC
Host Your Next Event
at CHASE FIELD 602-462-6455
chasefieldevents.com
STADIUM
D-BACKS
ROCKIES
IS THIS YOUR LUCKY DAY?
FRIDAY'S Front Row SPORTS GRILL
LEXUS
CHASE
GEICO
BUD LIGHT
NLCS 2007

Home Turf

The Diamondbacks have played in the same stadium since they joined the NL in 1998. It was only the second ballpark in baseball with a *retractable* roof and the first to have natural grass underneath such a roof. Summer days are very hot in Arizona. The Diamondbacks keep the roof open until three hours before game time so the grass gets sunlight. Then the roof is closed so that the air conditioning can cool the stadium. Each game, a few lucky fans can also beat the heat by jumping into the swimming pool located behind the right field wall.

The Diamondbacks' stadium was called Bank One Ballpark when it opened. Fans thought it was easier to use its initials, so they called it the "BOB." That changed in 2007 when Chase Bank bought Bank One. The team switched the stadium's name to Chase Field.

BY THE NUMBERS

- The Diamondbacks' stadium has 48,569 seats.
- The distance from home plate to the left field foul pole is 330 feet.
- The distance from home plate to the center field fence is 407 feet.
- The distance from home plate to the right field foul pole is 334 feet.

The roof is open at Arizona's stadium during a game in October for the 2007 NL championship.

Dressed for Success

For their first nine seasons, the Diamondbacks used three main colors—blue, brown, and purple. The blue was a shade called turquoise, which is a beautiful stone found in Arizona. The brown was meant to *represent* copper. Arizona is the nation's number-one copper producer. The purple was the same color worn by the Phoenix Suns basketball team. It had become a popular color in Arizona sports.

The team's *logo* featured a large letter *A*. Arizona's cap used a snake *symbol*. It showed a rattlesnake shaped like the letter *D*, for Diamondbacks.

In 2007, the Diamondbacks unveiled a new uniform. The big letters *A* and *D* were still there, but the team changed its main colors to Sedona Red and Sonora Sand. Sedona is the name of a city that is surrounded by beautiful red rocks. Sonora is the name of a desert in Arizona. The uniforms also use the team's nickname, "D-backs."

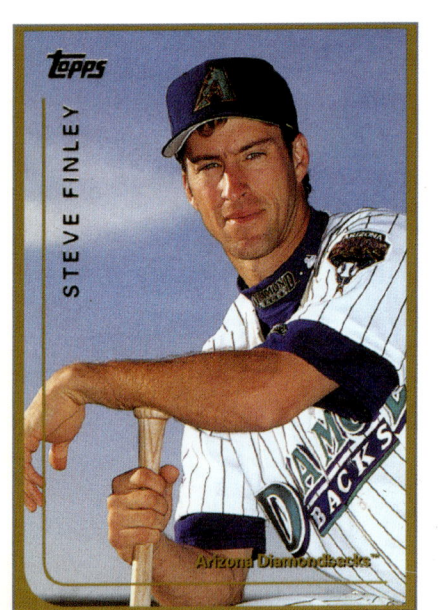

Steve Finley models the uniform Arizona wore in its early years.

UNIFORM BASICS

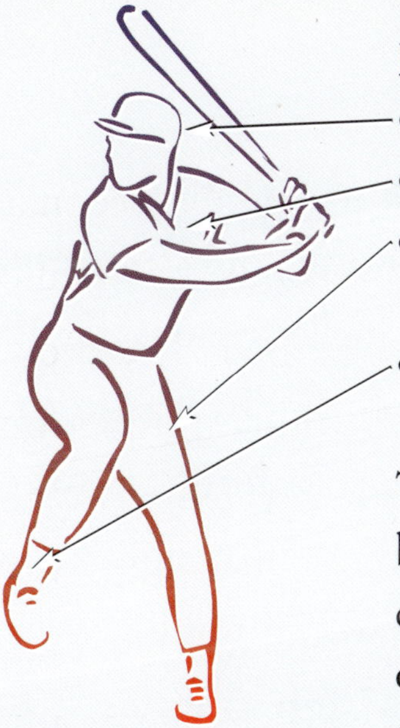

The baseball uniform has not changed much since the Diamondbacks began playing. It has four main parts:
- a cap or batting helmet with a sun visor
- a top with a player's number on the back
- pants that reach down between the ankle and the knee
- stirrup-style socks

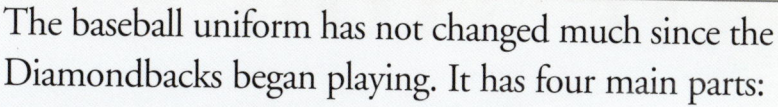

The uniform top sometimes has a player's name on the back. The team's name, city, or logo is usually on the front. Baseball teams wear light-colored uniforms when they play at home and darker styles when they play on the road.

For more than 100 years, baseball uniforms were made of wool *flannel* and were very baggy. This helped the sweat *evaporate* and gave players the freedom to move around. Today's uniforms are made of *synthetic* fabrics that stretch with players and keep them dry and cool.

Stephen Drew rounds the bases in the uniform the Diamondbacks unveiled in 2007.

We Won!

Baseball fans considered the 2001 Diamondbacks an old team. The average age of the players was 32. However, only one player on the club had ever won a World Series. The challenge for Arizona's new manager, Bob Brenly, was to turn the Diamondbacks' hunger for a World Series ring into an actual championship. It would not be easy.

In the **Division Series**, the Diamondbacks battled the St. Louis Cardinals down to the final inning of the final game. Curt Schilling had pitched a **shutout** in the opening game of the series for Arizona. Now, going into the ninth inning of Game Five, he was exhausted. Though the Cardinals had just scored the tying run, Brenly decided to keep his star pitcher in the game. Schilling held St. Louis for three more outs, and then the Diamondbacks took over with their bats. They won in the bottom of the inning on a bloop single by Tony Womack.

Next up in the **National League Championship Series (NLCS)** were the Atlanta Braves. In a duel between baseball's best **pitching staffs**, the Diamondbacks came out on top, four games to one. Schilling and Miguel Batista each recorded a victory, and Randy Johnson won two times to lead Arizona to its first pennant.

The World Series matched Arizona against the New York Yankees. The Diamondbacks won the first two games in front of their home fans. Johnson and Schilling gave up a total of one run, while their teammates scored 13 times. For once, it looked like the D-backs might have it easy.

LEFT: Curt Schilling, the hero of Game Five in the Division Series.
ABOVE: Randy Johnson celebrates after his victory in Game Two of the World Series.

The series moved to New York, where the Yankees felt very confident. They won Game Three by a score of 2–1. In Game Four, Schilling was cruising along with a two-run lead when Brenly decided to remove him. The Diamondbacks were stunned when Byung-Hyun Kim gave up home runs to Tino Martinez and Derek Jeter to lose the game in the 10th inning. The next night, Kim was called in again to protect a two-run lead. This time, he gave up a game-tying home run to Scott Brosius. The Yankees won in the 12th inning.

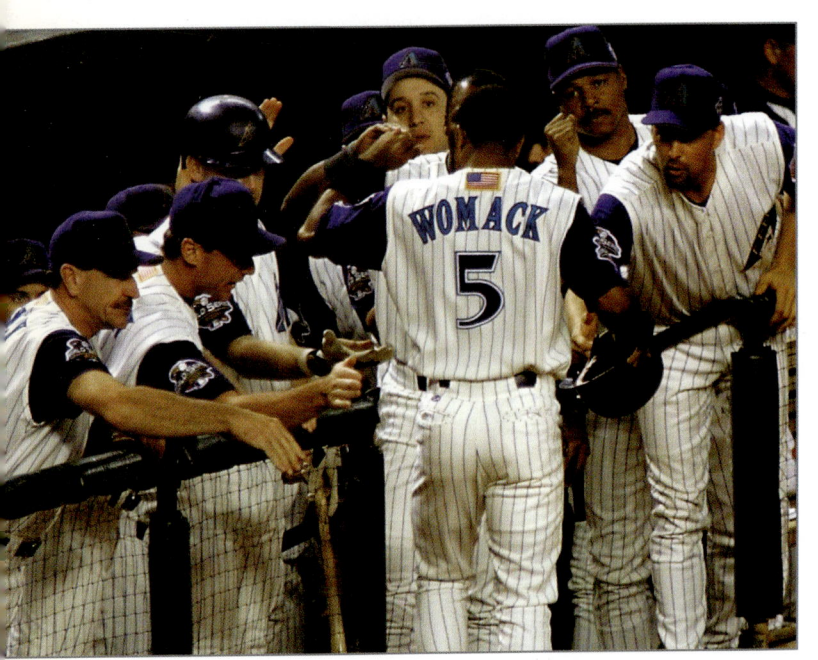

The two teams returned to Arizona to finish the series. The Diamondbacks had to win twice. In Game Six, they destroyed the Yankees with 15 runs and 22 hits. Some fans were worried that the Arizona offense might struggle the following night in Game Seven. At first, it looked that way.

Schilling and Roger Clemens of the Yankees pitched brilliantly. The Diamondbacks got one run off of Clemens in the sixth inning, but New York scored in the seventh and eighth to take a 2–1 lead. The Yankees

ABOVE: Teammates congratulate Tony Womack during Arizona's blowout win in Game Six.   **RIGHT**: Luis Gonzalez jumps for joy after his winning hit in Game Seven.

then sent Mariano Rivera to the mound. He was the best **closer** in baseball.

The Diamondbacks would not back down. Mark Grace led off the ninth with a single to center field. David Dellucci replaced him as a **pinch-runner**. Damian Miller bunted, and Rivera made a bad throw to second. Dellucci was safe. Next up was Jay Bell, who also bunted. This time, Rivera pounced off the mound and threw out Dellucci at third base.

Womack walked to the plate next for Arizona. Brenly let him swing away. Womack responded with a double to tie the score at 2–2. With runners on second and third, Rivera hit Craig Counsell with a pitch to load the bases.

Into the batter's box stepped Luis Gonzalez. The fans in Arizona rose to their feet. The stadium had never been noisier. Rivera's second pitch was a fastball that darted to the inside corner of home plate. Gonzalez swung, and the ball climbed softly in the air and floated over Jeter's head at shortstop. Bell came home with the winning run. The Diamondbacks were world champions!

Go-To Guys

To be a true star in baseball, you need more than a quick bat and a strong arm. You have to be a "go-to guy"—someone the manager wants on the pitcher's mound or in the batter's box when it matters most. Fans of the Diamondbacks have had a lot to cheer about over the years, including these great stars ...

THE PIONEERS

JAY BELL — Second Baseman/Shortstop

- BORN: 12/11/1965 • PLAYED FOR TEAM: 1998 TO 2002

Jay Bell was one of the friendliest, smartest players in the game. The Diamondbacks got him to set an example for their younger stars. In 1999, he hit 38 home runs and became an **All-Star**.

LUIS GONZALEZ — Outfielder

- BORN: 9/3/1967
- PLAYED FOR TEAM: 1999 TO 2006

Luis Gonzalez was a good hitter during his first 10 years in the big leagues. He became a great one after he joined the Diamondbacks. "Gonzo" led the NL in hits in 1999 and smashed 57 home runs in 2001.

ABOVE: Jay Bell **TOP RIGHT**: Steve Finley
BOTTOM RIGHT: Randy Johnson and Curt Schilling

STEVE FINLEY   Outfielder

- BORN: 3/12/1965
- PLAYED FOR TEAM: 1999 TO 2004

Steve Finley was another experienced star who loved playing in Arizona. He was an excellent center fielder and hit 69 home runs in his first two years as a D-back.

RANDY JOHNSON   Pitcher

- BORN: 9/10/1963
- PLAYED FOR TEAM: 1999 TO 2004; RETURNED TO TEAM IN 2007

Randy Johnson was the greatest pitcher in Arizona history. The "Big Unit" led the NL in strikeouts five times and won the **Cy Young Award** in each of his first four seasons with the team. In 2001, Johnson struck out 20 batters in a game.

CURT SCHILLING   Pitcher

- BORN: 11/14/1966
- PLAYED FOR TEAM: 2000 TO 2003

Arizona traded four young players to get Curt Schilling, and he was worth the price. Schilling won 22 games in 2001 and had four more victories in the playoffs and World Series. In 2002, he and Randy Johnson became the first teammates to each strike out 300 batters in the same season.

MODERN STARS

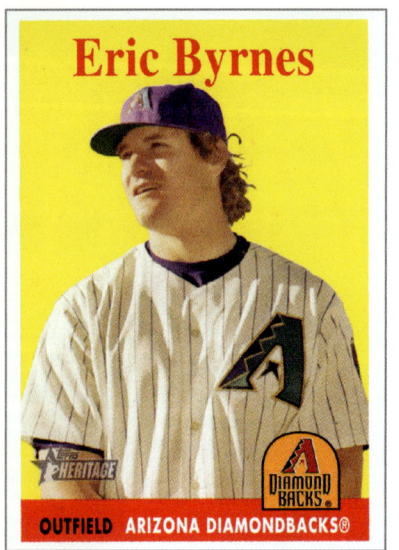

JOSE VALVERDE — Pitcher

- BORN: 7/24/1979
- PLAYED FOR TEAM: 2003 TO 2007

Hard-throwing Jose Valverde was one of the best **relief pitchers** in baseball from the moment he joined the Diamondbacks. In 2007, after recovering from an arm injury, he **saved** 47 games.

BRANDON WEBB — Pitcher

- BORN: 5/9/1979
- FIRST YEAR WITH TEAM: 2003

Brandon Webb used a great sinking fastball to become Arizona's best pitcher. In 2006, he tied for the NL lead in wins and shutouts, and won the Cy Young Award.

ERIC BYRNES — Outfielder

- BORN: 2/16/1976
- FIRST YEAR WITH TEAM: 2006

The Diamondbacks won the 2001 World Series thanks to their veteran leaders. They signed Eric Byrnes in 2006 to give them that same kind of spark. He did everything well on and off the field, and played as hard as anyone in the game.

STEPHEN DREW　　　　Shortstop

- BORN: 3/16/1983　• FIRST YEAR WITH TEAM: 2006

When Stephen Drew broke in with Arizona in 2006, his older brother J.D. was already a big-league star. The younger Drew quickly made a name for himself with his clutch hitting and strong leadership.

CHRIS YOUNG　　　　Outfielder

- BORN: 9/5/1983　• FIRST YEAR WITH TEAM: 2006

Chris Young started his career as a **leadoff hitter**. By the end of the 2007 season, the Diamondbacks realized that he could be a great power hitter, too. Young hit 32 home runs and stole 27 bases in his first full year with Arizona.

JUSTIN UPTON　　　　Outfielder

- BORN: 8/25/1987　• FIRST YEAR WITH TEAM: 2007

Early in 2007, Arizona fans were calling minor leaguer Justin Upton their "right fielder of the future." The future arrived sooner than expected. Upton took over the job in August of that season and showed the *potential* to be a star.

TOP LEFT: Brandon Webb
BOTTOM LEFT: Eric Byrnes
TOP RIGHT: Stephen Drew and Chris Young
BOTTOM RIGHT: Justin Upton

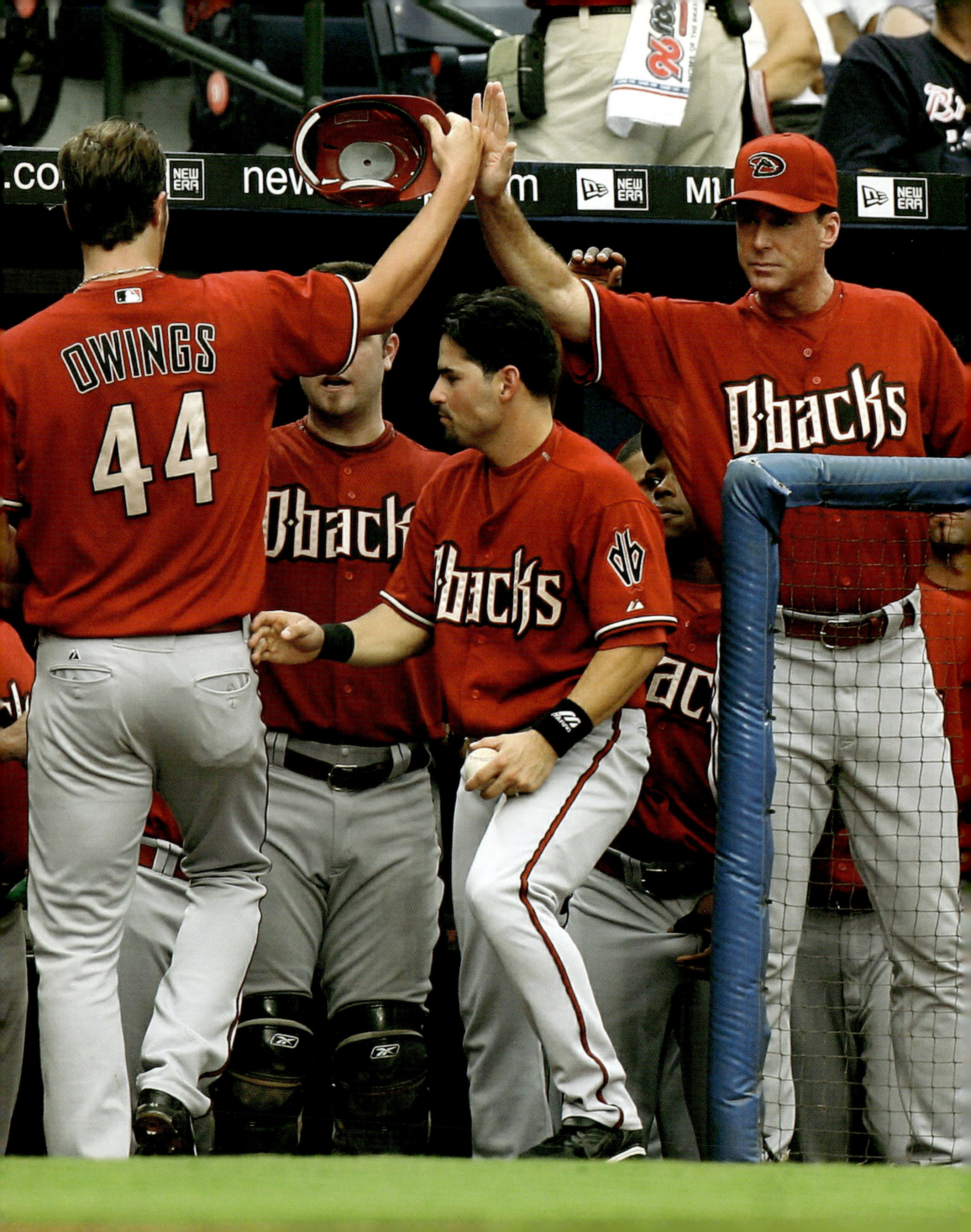
NEW ERA
NEW ERA
NEW ERA
OWINGS
44
Dbacks
Dbacks
Dbacks

On the Sidelines

When the Diamondbacks first formed, they immediately hired Buck Showalter to put together their club. He had helped build the New York Yankees into a championship team in the 1990s and was the American League's Manager of the Year in 1994. Showalter eventually left the Diamondbacks, but his contributions were felt on the Arizona club that won the 2001 World Series.

The manager of that championship team was Bob Brenly. He became just the third **rookie** manager to win a World Series. Brenly had been a power-hitting catcher as a player, and he was very good at working with pitchers. Of course, having Randy Johnson and Curt Schilling made his job a lot easier!

In 2005, the Diamondbacks hired Bob Melvin to manage the team. Like Brenly, he was a former catcher. Melvin was also a coach for Brenly on the 2001 Diamondbacks. Arizona **entrusted** him with the development of the team's new stars. He led the D-backs to the NL West title in just his third season.

Bob Melvin greets Micah Owings in the dugout with a high five. Melvin was named the NL Manager of the Year in 2007.

One Great Day

MAY 18, 2004

Whenever Randy Johnson pitched for the Diamondbacks, there was always a chance that he would treat fans to a truly special performance. That is one of the reasons why a crowd of more than 20,000 showed up at Turner Field in Atlanta on a Tuesday night in May 2004.

The Diamondbacks were in a rebuilding year. They would lose 111 games during the season. Outside of Johnson, there was not much to see. But Braves fans still got their money's worth that night.

Johnson made history against Atlanta. Inning after inning, he set down the opposing hitters 1–2–3. Johnson was pouring sizzling fastballs over the plate. Most of the Braves had two strikes on them before they knew it. Johnson struck out 13 Atlanta batters in all.

Johnson's fastball got stronger as the game went on. His curve and slider were bending sharply as they reached home plate. A few Braves hit the ball hard, but the closest Atlanta came to a hit was a weak grounder by its pitcher, Mike Hampton. Alex Cintron scooped up the roller, and his throw to first arrived a half-step before Hampton.

The Diamondbacks mob Randy Johnson after the last out of his perfect game.

The 27th batter for the Braves was a **pinch-hitter**, Eddie Perez. Johnson struck him out with a 98 mph fastball. It was a perfect game—only the 16th in history. Johnson pumped his fist and celebrated as his teammates surrounded him on the mound.

The Diamondbacks had a rare 2–0 victory, and Johnson's perfect game was also his second **no-hitter**. His first had come 14 years earlier, in 1990. The Atlanta fans gave him a standing ovation as he walked into the dugout.

"This is one of those nights where a *superior* athlete was on top of his game," said Arizona manager Bob Brenly. "There was a tremendous rhythm out there. His focus, his concentration, his stuff—everything was as good as it could possibly be."

Johnson soon learned that, at age 40, he was the oldest pitcher to throw a perfect game. The record had been held by 37-year-old Cy Young. Johnson knew something about that baseball legend. He had five Cy Young Awards in his trophy case.

Legend Has It

Who was the most superstitious Diamondback?

LEGEND HAS IT that Brandon Webb was. Most baseball players do not like to change their daily routines when things are going well. Webb is no exception. The morning of every game he starts, Webb has to eat pancakes. That is because he ate at the International House of Pancakes before each of his 16 victories in 2006, the year he won the Cy Young Award.

ABOVE: Brandon Webb   **RIGHT**: The Diamondbacks celebrate after Game Seven of the 2001 World Series.

Was Arizona's ninth-inning comeback in 2001 the best ever in a World Series?

LEGEND HAS IT that it was. When the Diamondbacks came to bat in the bottom of the ninth inning of Game Seven, they trailed the New York Yankees by one run. No team had ever been in that situation in the World Series and won. Arizona scored twice to take the championship.

Who was the first Diamondback to be honored by the Hall of Fame?

LEGEND HAS IT that Greg Colbrunn was. In Game Six of the 2001 World Series, Colbrunn hit a single against the Yankees. It was Arizona's 21st hit—a new record for a World Series game. The **Hall of Fame** asked for the baseball, and it is stored in Cooperstown today.

It Really Happened

In Arizona's second season, the team and a company called Shamrock Farms held a contest together. Every Sunday would be "**Grand Slam** Sunday." A fan would be picked at *random* and asked to name a player and an inning. If that player hit a grand slam in that inning, the fan would win $1 million.

Gylene Hoyle was a Diamondbacks fan, but she had never been to a game. She decided to call a local radio station during a contest and was lucky enough to win a ticket to that Sunday's game against the Oakland A's. As Hoyle entered the stadium, her good luck continued. She was picked for the Shamrock Farms contest.

Hoyle predicted that her favorite player, Jay Bell, would hit a grand slam during the sixth inning. When Bell came to bat in the fifth inning, Hoyle became nervous. It did not look as if Bell would have a chance to hit in the sixth.

But fate was still smiling on Hoyle. In the next inning, two doubles and two walks brought Bell to the plate with the bases loaded and two outs. Hoyle's pick had been announced to the crowd. The fans were screaming as Oakland pitcher Jimmy Haynes peered in from the mound. Bell worked the count to three balls and

Jay Bell circles the bases after hitting a home run.

one strike. He took good swings at the next two pitches and hit them both foul. The crowd grew louder and louder with each pitch.

Then, what seemed impossible happened. Haynes threw one down the middle, Bell met the ball with a smooth swing, and it soared toward left field. Outfielder Tim Raines ran to the wall and thought he might catch the drive. When the ball landed in the seats, the stadium **erupted** in a wild celebration. Hoyle was a millionaire, and 36,000 fans had just **witnessed** the craziest moment in the team's short history.

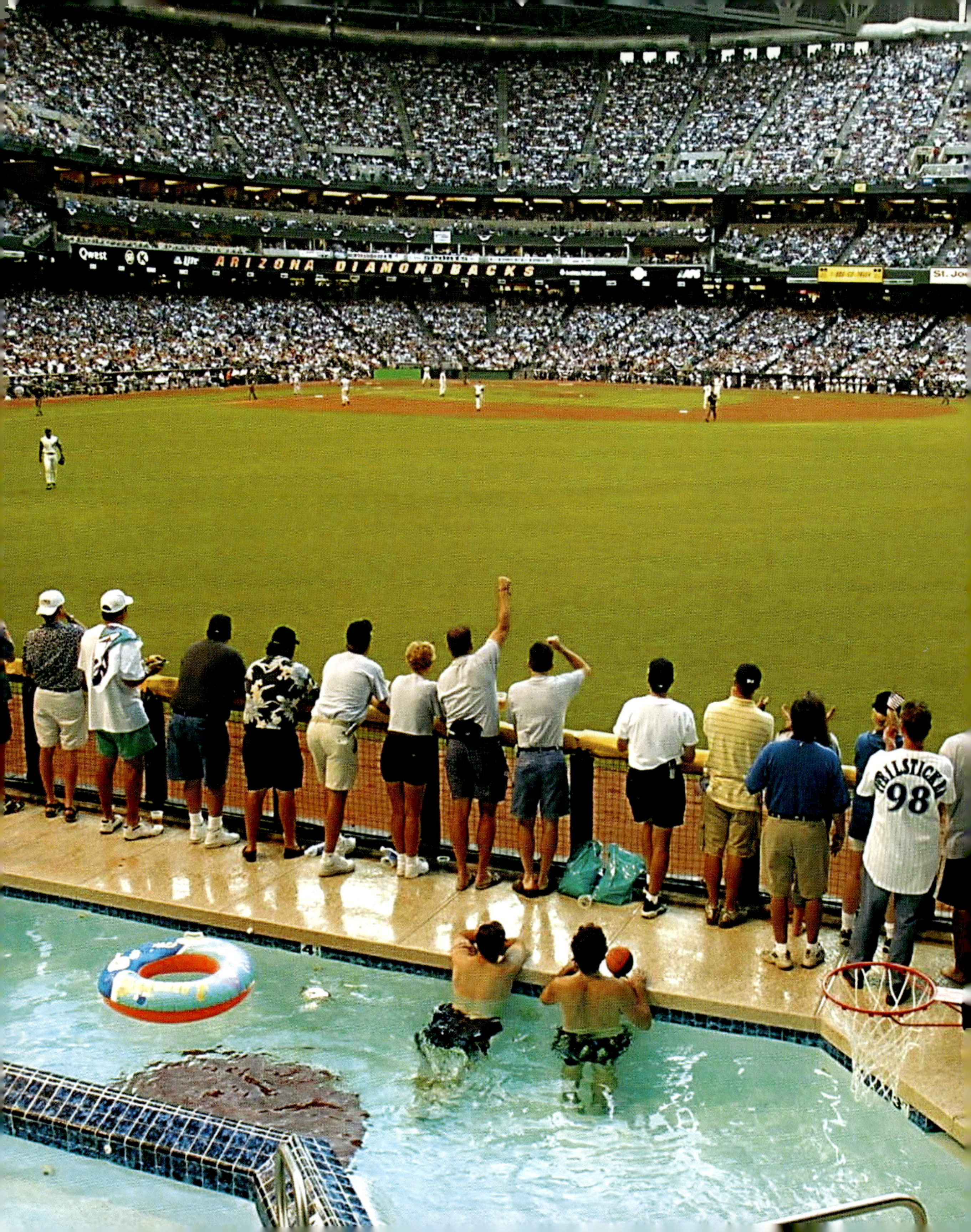
ARIZONA DIAMONDBACKS
Qwest
98

Team Spirit

The Diamondbacks made a promise to their fans in 1998. The team said it would do whatever it took to compete for the pennant. Arizona kept its promise, and the Diamondbacks built a good team quickly. They were NL West champions in 1999 and world champions in 2001. After their World Series victory, the Diamondbacks held a parade. More than 300,000 fans came to celebrate Arizona's first major-league sports championship.

Not surprisingly, the Diamondbacks get large and *enthusiastic* crowds at their games. For many years, the team sold tickets in the upper deck for $1. Those seats were very popular. But the "coolest" spot in the stadium is located behind the fence in right field. There, on a warm night or day, fans can enjoy a large swimming pool. Also behind the outfield fence is the Peter Piper Playhouse, which has a lot of games for families.

At Diamondbacks games, fans can take a dip and catch the action on the field at the same time.

Timeline

Steve Finley

1999
Steve Finley becomes the first Diamondback to win a **Gold Glove Award**.

2001
Arizona defeats the New York Yankees to win the World Series.

1998
The Diamondbacks play their first season.

2000
Tony Womack leads the league with 14 triples.

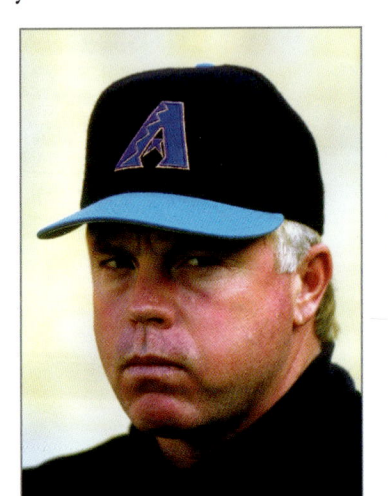

Buck Showalter, Arizona's first manager.

Tony Womack

Brandon Webb delivers a pitch during his Cy Young season.

2004
Randy Johnson pitches a perfect game.

2006
Brandon Webb wins the Cy Young Award.

2002
Randy Johnson leads the NL in wins, strikeouts, and **earned run average (ERA)**.

2007
The Diamondbacks win the NL West for the fourth time.

Randy Johnson

The D-backs celebrate their 2007 title.

Fun Facts

BIRD HUNTING
The Diamondbacks have scored 17 runs in a game against the St. Louis Cardinals three times—in 1999, 2000, and 2001.

BREAKFAST CLUB
On the day tickets for Arizona's first game went on sale in January 1998, they were gone by lunchtime.

ALL IN THE FAMILY
Conor Jackson is not the first famous person in his family. His father, John, is a television and movie actor.

K FACTOR
In 2002, Randy Johnson became the first pitcher to reach 300 strikeouts (or "Ks") in a season five times in a row.

ABOVE: Conor Jackson
RIGHT: Tony Clark

STRETCH

First baseman Tony Clark looked familiar to a lot of Arizona fans when he joined the team in 2005. Years earlier, he had played college basketball for the University of Arizona.

HE'S NO SCRUB

Brandon Webb's nickname is "Sponge." He loves to soak up as much information from teammates as he can.

GOING, GOING, GONZO!

One of the hardest things to do as a hitter is to finish the year with 100 extra-base hits (doubles, triples, and home runs). In 2001, Luis Gonzalez hit 57 homers, 36 doubles, and seven triples to record exactly 100.

NICE PICK

The best player chosen by Arizona in the 1997 **expansion draft** was David Dellucci. He became the first Diamondback to lead the league in a major category. Dellucci hit an NL-best 12 triples in 1998.

Talking Baseball

"I had to come in and ask all these guys who had accomplished these great things as individuals, to stop thinking as individuals. They had to think as a unit."
—*Bob Brenly, on his greatest challenge as a rookie manager in 2001*

"I throw the sinker 80, 85, 90 percent of the time. Even though they know it's coming, it's still tough to lift the ball up. Most of the time they just knock it on the ground."
—*Brandon Webb, on the secret to retiring good hitters*

"When you win, you want more of it. You can't win enough."
—*Randy Johnson, on what kept him pitching into his 40s*

"I don't have the best skills, but I'm going to give it everything I've got. It's not always been pretty, but there's something to be said for guys that play in the league for a long time and know how to get the job done."
—*Luis Gonzalez, on the value of experience and hard work*

"Have fun and remember—if you are going to make a mistake, make sure you make it being aggressive."
—*Eric Byrnes, on being a hardworking player*

"I'm a pretty ugly guy, and it's a pretty ugly doll, so I think they did a good job of capturing my likeness."
—*Mark Grace, on the bobblehead doll of him given to fans in 2001*

"It was a magical time and an unbelievable World Series. An important time in our country after 9/11. Just to be a part of it, win or lose, was an experience that can never be **duplicated**."
—*Craig Counsell, on the 2001 World Series*

LEFT: Bob Brenly   **ABOVE**: Mark Grace and Craig Counsell celebrate in the locker room after the 2001 World Series.

For the Record

The great Diamondbacks teams and players have left their marks on the record books. These are the "best of the best"…

DIAMONDBACKS AWARD WINNERS

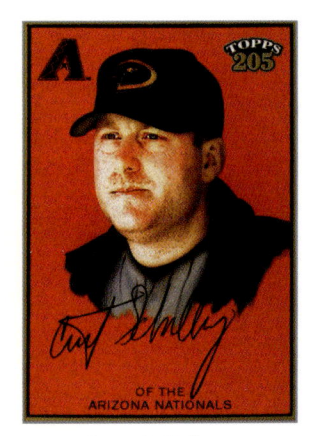

WINNER	AWARD	YEAR
Randy Johnson	Cy Young Award	1999
Randy Johnson	Cy Young Award	2000
Randy Johnson	Cy Young Award	2001
Curt Schilling	World Series co-MVP	2001
Randy Johnson	World Series co-MVP	2001
Randy Johnson	Cy Young Award	2002
Brandon Webb	Cy Young Award	2006
Bob Melvin	Manager of the Year	2007

Curt Schilling

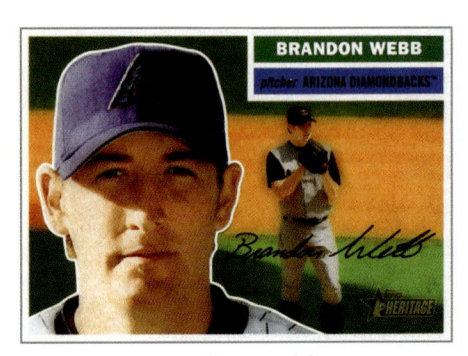

Brandon Webb

Randy Johnson

DIAMONDBACKS ACHIEVEMENTS

ACHIEVEMENT	YEAR
NL West Champions	1999
NL West Champions	2001
NL Pennant Winners	2001
World Series Champions	2001
NL West Champions	2002
NL West Champions	2007

LEFT: Jose Valverde, closer for the 2007 club. Reggie Sanders (**TOP**) and Damian Miller (**BOTTOM**), key members of the 2001 champs.

Pinpoints

The history of a baseball team is made up of many smaller stories. These stories take place all over the map—not just in the city a team calls "home." Match the pushpins on these maps to the Team Facts and you will begin to see the story of the Diamondbacks unfold!

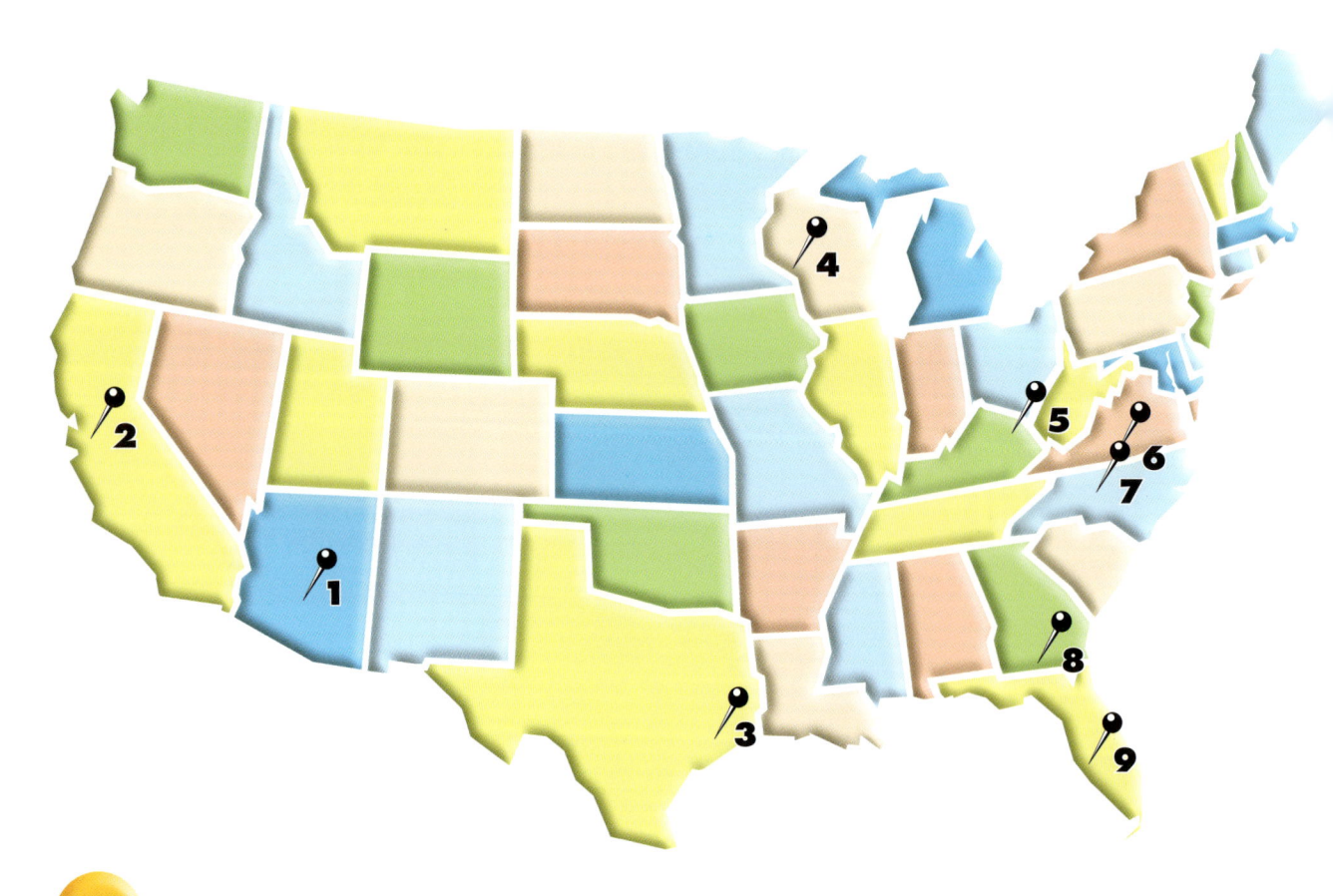

TEAM FACTS

1 Phoenix, Arizona—*The team has played here since 1998.*
2 Walnut Creek, California—*Randy Johnson was born here.*
3 Houston, Texas—*Chris Young was born here.*
4 La Crosse, Wisconsin—*Damian Miller was born here.*
5 Ashland, Kentucky—*Brandon Webb was born here.*
6 Chatham, Virginia—*Tony Womack was born here.*
7 Winston-Salem, North Carolina—*Mark Grace was born here.*
8 Hahira, Georgia—*Stephen Drew was born here.*
9 Tampa, Florida—*Luis Gonzalez was born here.*
10 Anchorage, Alaska—*Curt Schilling was born here.*
11 San Pedro de Macoris, Dominican Republic—*Jose Valverde was born here.*
12 Kwangju, South Korea—*Byung-Hyun Kim was born here.*

Byung-Hyun Kim

Play Ball

Baseball is a game played between two teams over nine innings. Teams take one turn at bat and one turn in the field during each inning. A turn at bat ends when three outs are made. The batters on the hitting team try to reach base safely. The players on the fielding team try to prevent this from happening.

In baseball, the ball is controlled by the pitcher. The pitcher must throw the ball to the batter, who decides whether or not to swing at each pitch. If a batter swings and misses, it is a strike. If the batter lets a good pitch go by, it is also a strike. If the batter swings and the ball does not stay in fair territory (between the v-shaped lines that begin at home plate) it is called "foul," and is counted as a strike. If the pitcher throws three strikes, the batter is out. If the pitcher throws four bad pitches before that, the batter is awarded first base. This is called a base-on-balls, or "walk."

When the batter swings the bat and hits the ball, everyone springs into action. If a fielder catches a batted ball before it hits the ground, the batter is out. If a fielder scoops the ball off the ground and throws it to first base before the batter arrives, the batter is out. If the batter reaches first base safely, he is credited with a hit. A one-base hit is called a single, a two-base hit is called a double, a three-base hit is called a triple, and a four-base hit is called a home run.

Runners who reach base are only safe when they are touching one of the bases. If they are caught between the bases, the fielders can tag them with the ball and record an out.

A batter who is able to circle the bases and make it back to home plate before three outs are made is credited with a run scored. The team with the most runs after nine innings is the winner.

Anyone who has played baseball (or softball) knows that it can be a complicated game. Every player on the field has a job to do. Different players have different strengths and weaknesses. The pitchers, batters, and managers make hundreds of decisions every game. The more you play and watch baseball, the more "little things" you are likely to notice. The next time you are at a game, look for these plays:

PLAY LIST

DOUBLE PLAY—A play where the fielding team is able to make two outs on one batted ball. This usually happens when a runner is on first base, and the batter hits a ground ball to one of the infielders. The base runner is forced out at second base and the ball is then thrown to first base before the batter arrives.

HIT AND RUN—A play where the runner on first base sprints to second base while the pitcher is throwing the ball to the batter. When the second baseman or shortstop moves toward the base to wait for the catcher's throw, the batter tries to hit the ball to the place that the fielder has just left. If the batter swings and misses, the fielding team can tag the runner out.

INTENTIONAL WALK—A play when the pitcher throws four bad pitches on purpose, allowing the batter to walk to first base. This happens when the pitcher would much rather face the next batter—and is willing to risk putting a runner on base.

SACRIFICE BUNT—A play where the batter makes an out on purpose so that a teammate can move to the next base. On a bunt, the batter tries to "deaden" the pitch with the bat instead of swinging at it.

SHOESTRING CATCH—A play where an outfielder catches a short hit an inch or two above the ground, near the tops of his shoes. It is not easy to run as fast as you can and lower your glove without slowing down. It can be risky, too. If a fielder misses a shoestring catch, the ball might roll all the way to the fence.

Glossary

BASEBALL WORDS TO KNOW

ALL-STAR—A player who is selected to play in baseball's annual All-Star Game.

CLOSER—A pitcher who finishes close games.

CY YOUNG AWARD—The annual trophy given to each league's best pitcher.

DIVISION SERIES—A series played to determine which teams have a chance to advance to the World Series.

EARNED RUN AVERAGE (ERA)—A statistic that counts how many runs a pitcher gives up for every nine innings he pitches.

EXPANSION DRAFT—A meeting where teams new to a league get to select players from other teams.

EXPANSION TEAM—A new team added to a league.

GOLD GLOVE AWARD—An award given each year to baseball's best fielders.

GRAND SLAM—A home run with the bases loaded.

HALL OF FAME—The museum in Cooperstown, New York, where baseball's greatest players are honored. A player voted into the Hall of Fame is sometimes called a "Hall of Famer."

LEADOFF HITTER—The first hitter in a lineup, or the first hitter in an inning.

MINOR LEAGUES—The many professional leagues that help develop players for the major leagues.

MOST VALUABLE PLAYER (MVP)—An award given each year to each league's top player; an MVP is also selected for the World Series and All-Star Game.

NATIONAL LEAGUE (NL)—The older of the two major leagues; the NL began play in 1876 and the American League (AL) started in 1901.

NATIONAL LEAGUE CHAMPIONSHIP SERIES (NLCS)—The competition that has decided the National League pennant since 1969.

NL WEST—A group of National League teams that plays in the western part of the country.

NO-HITTER—A game in which a team is unable to get a hit.

PENNANT—A league championship. The term comes from the triangular flag awarded to each season's champion, beginning in the 1870s.

PINCH-HITTER—A player who is sent into the game to hit for a teammate.

PINCH-RUNNER—A player who is sent into the game to run for a teammate.

PITCHING STAFFS—The groups of players who pitch for teams.

PROSPECTS—Young players who are expected to become stars.

RELIEF PITCHERS—Substitute pitchers.

ROOKIE—Someone in his first season.

RUNS BATTED IN (RBI)—A statistic that counts the number of runners a batter drives home.

SAVED—Recorded the last out in a team's win.

SHUTOUT—A game in which one team does not allow its opponent to score a run.

STARTING PITCHER—The pitcher who begins the game for his team.

VETERANS—Players who have great experience.

WORLD SERIES—The world championship series played between the winners of the National League and American League.

OTHER WORDS TO KNOW

DOMINATED—Controlled completely through the use of power.

DUPLICATED—Repeated.

ENTHUSIASTIC—Filled with strong excitement.

ENTRUSTED—Gave someone the responsibility of care and protection.

ERUPTED—Burst suddenly.

EVAPORATE—Disappear, or turn into vapor.

EXPERIENCED—Having knowledge and skill in a job.

FLANNEL—A soft wool or cotton material.

GENERATION—A period of years roughly equal to the time it takes for a person to be born, grow up, and have children.

INSISTED—Stated forcefully.

LOGO—A symbol or design that represents a company or team.

PATIENT—Able to wait calmly.

POTENTIAL—Capable of becoming better.

RANDOM—Lacking a plan or pattern.

REPRESENT—To act, speak, or stand for something.

RETRACTABLE—Able to pull back.

STRATEGY—A plan or method for succeeding.

SUPERIOR—The very best.

SYMBOL—Something that represents a thought or idea.

SYNTHETIC—Made in a laboratory, not in nature.

TRADITION—A belief or custom that is handed down from generation to generation.

WITNESSED—Watched something happen.

Places to Go

ON THE ROAD

ARIZONA DIAMONDBACKS
401 East Jefferson Street
Phoenix, Arizona 85004
(520) 434-1367

NATIONAL BASEBALL HALL OF FAME AND MUSEUM
25 Main Street
Cooperstown, New York 13326
(888) 425-5633
www.baseballhalloffame.org

ON THE WEB

THE ARIZONA DIAMONDBACKS www.arizonadiamondbacks.com
  • *Learn more about the Diamondbacks*

MAJOR LEAGUE BASEBALL www.mlb.com
  • *Learn more about all the major league teams*

MINOR LEAGUE BASEBALL www.minorleaguebaseball.com
  • *Learn more about the minor leagues*

ON THE BOOKSHELF

To learn more about the sport of baseball, look for these books at your library or bookstore:

- Kelly, James. *Baseball*. New York, New York: DK, 2005.
- Jacobs, Greg. *The Everything Kids' Baseball Book*. Cincinnati, Ohio: Adams Media Corporation, 2006.
- Stewart, Mark and Kennedy, Mike. *Long Ball: The Legend and Lore of the Home Run*. Minneapolis, Minnesota: Millbrook Press, 2006.

Index

PAGE NUMBERS IN **BOLD** REFER TO ILLUSTRATIONS.

Bank One Ballpark 13	Johnson, Randy 7, **8**, 9,
Batista, Miguel 7, 17	17, **17**, 21, **21**,
Bell, Jay 6, 19, 20, **20**, 30, 31, **31**	25, 26, 27, **27**, 35,
Benes, Andy 6	**35**, 36, 38, 40, **40**, 43
Brenly, Bob 16, 17, 18,	Kim, Byung-Hyun 18, 43, **43**
19, 25, 27, 38, **38**	Knight, Philip 6
Brosius, Scott 18	Manning, Danny 6
Byrnes, Eric 11, 22, **22**, 39	Martinez, Tino 18
Chase Field **12**, 13	Melvin, Bob **24**, 25, 40
Cintron, Alex 26	Miller, Damian 19, **41**, 43
Clark, Tony 37, **37**	Montero, Miguel 11
Clemens, Roger 18	Perez, Eddie 27
Colangelo, Jerry 6, **6**	Owings, Micah 11, 24
Colbrunn, Greg 29	Quentin, Carlos 11
Counsell, Craig 7, 19, 39, **39**	Raines, Tim 31
Crystal, Billy 6	Reynolds, Mark 11
Dellucci, David 19, 37	Rivera, Mariano 19
Drew, J.D. 23	Sanders, Reggie 7, **41**
Drew, Stephen 11, **15**,	Schilling, Curt 7, 9, **9**,
23, **23**, 43	16, **16**, 17, 18,
Finley, Steve 7, 9, **14**,	21, **21**, 25, 40, **40**, 43
21, **21**, 34, **34**	Showalter, Buck 25, **34**
Gonzalez, Edgar 11	Tracy, Chad 11
Gonzalez, Luis 7, 7, 9,	Upton, Justin **10**, 11, 23, **23**
19, **19**, 20, 37, 39, 43	Valverde, Jose 11, 22, **41**, 43
Grace, Mark 7, 19, 39, **39**, 43	Webb, Brandon 9, 11, 22,
Hampton, Mike 26	22, 28, **28**, 35,
Haynes, Jimmy 30, 31	**35**, 37, 38, 40, **40**, 43
Hernandez, Livan 11	White, Devon 6
Hoyle, Gylene 30, 31	Williams, Matt 6
Hudson, Orlando 11	Womack, Tony 7, 9, 16,
Jackson, Conor 11, 36, **36**	**18**, 19, 34, **34**, 43
Jackson, John 36	Young, Chris **10** 11, 23, **23**, 43
Jeter, Derek 18, 19	Young, Cy 27

48

The Team

MARK STEWART has written more than 25 books on baseball, and over 100 sports books for kids. He grew up in New York City during the 1960s rooting for the Yankees and Mets, and now takes his two daughters, Mariah and Rachel, to the same ballparks. Mark comes from a family of writers. His grandfather was Sunday Editor of the *New York Times* and his mother was Articles Editor of *Ladies' Home Journal* and *McCall's*. Mark has profiled hundreds of athletes over the last 20 years. He has also written several books about his native New York and New Jersey, his home today. Mark is a graduate of Duke University, with a degree in history. He lives with his daughters and wife, Sarah, overlooking Sandy Hook, NJ.

JAMES L. GATES, JR. has served as Library Director at the National Baseball Hall of Fame since 1995. He had previously served in academic libraries for almost fifteen years. He holds degrees from Belmont Abbey College, the University of Notre Dame, and Indiana University. During his career Jim has authored several academic articles and has served in an editorial capacity on multiple book, magazine, and museum publications, and he also serves as host for the Annual Cooperstown Symposium on Baseball and American Culture. He is an ardent Baltimore Orioles fan and enjoys watching baseball with his wife and two children.